Panama & Costa Rica Travel Guide

Attractions, Eating, Drinking, Shopping & Places To Stay

Olivia Phillips

Copyright © 2014, Astute Press
All Rights Reserved.

No part of this publication may be reproduced, stored in a retrieval system, or transmitted, in any form or by any means without the prior written permission of the publisher, nor be otherwise circulated in any form of binding or cover other than that in which it is published and without similar condition being imposed on the subsequent purchaser.

If there are any errors or omissions in copyright acknowledgements the publisher will be pleased to insert the appropriate acknowledgement in any subsequent printing of this publication.

Although we have taken all reasonable care in researching this book we make no warranty about the accuracy or completeness of its content and disclaim all liability arising from its use

Table of Contents

Panama 6
   Culture 7
   Location & Orientation 9
   Climate & When to Visit 10

Sightseeing Highlights 11
   Panama City 11
      Panama Canal 12
      Miraflores Locks Visitor Center 13
      Amador Causeway 14
      Palacio de las Garzas 15
      Panama Viejo 16
   Taboga 17
   Lake Gatun 18
   Santa Catalina 19
   Coiba Island National Park 20
   Bocas del Toro 22
   David 24
      Boquete 25
      Volcan Baru 26
   Pearl Islands 27
   San Blas Islands 28

Recommendations for the Budget Traveler 29
   Places to Stay 29
      Central Park Hotel 29
      Metro Hotel Panama 30
      Hotel Residencial Cervantes 30
      Hotel Refugio de Montana 31
      Hotel Hibiscusgarden 32
   Places to Eat & Drink 33
      Lenos & Carbon 33
      Tinajas 33
      PaParrillada Jimmy 34
      Big Daddy's Grill, Boquete 35
      Super Gourmet Bocas 35
   Places to Shop 36

    Mola & other Kuna Handicrafts 36
    Reprosa 37
    Crafts in Panama 37
    Flamenco Shopping Plaza 38
    Karavan Gallery 39

Costa Rica 40
Culture 41
Location & Orientation 43
Climate & When to Visit 44

Sightseeing Highlights 46
Canopy & Zip-line Tours 46
Coffee & Chocolate Tours 48
Beaches 50
Arenal Volcano 51
Tortuguero Turtle Nesting Area 53
Monteverde Cloud Forest 55
Cerro Chiripo 56
Whitewater Rafting 58
Museums of San Jose 59
Puerto Viejo de Talamanca 60

Recommendations for the Budget Traveler 63
Places to Stay 63
    Tree Houses Hotel near Arenal 63
    Casa Batsu in the Monteverde Cloud Forest 65
    Hotel Banana Azul in Puerto Viejo 66
    Adventure Inn in San Jose 66
    Casa Mariposa in Chirripo 67
Places to Eat & Drink 67
    Jardin del Parque in San Jose 68
    Stashus con Fusion in Puerto Viejo 68
    Restaurante Tico y Rico Monteverde 69
    Wild Ginger in Torguguero 69
    Cascajo's del Arenal 70
Places to Shop 70
    Mercado Central in San Jose 70
    Mercado Nacional de Artesanías in San Jose 71
    Multiplaza Mall in San Jose 71
    Roadside Market in Puerto Viejo 72
    Santa Elena Souvenir Shops in Monteverde 72

Panama

North and South America meet on the narrow isthmus known as Panama. Intriguingly, this is also where east met west in the early 16th century with the arrival of the Spanish Conquistadors, for whom Panama provided a gateway to Aztec and Inca riches. In the natural world, Panama also is a melting pot of biodiversity, a rare strip of land where the divergent species of the two Americas meet and mingle.

The versatile terrain provides a suitable arena for a variety of activities ranging from zip-lining, diving, surfing, fishing and sailing. Panama also has a modern cityscape and access to a rich patchwork of indigenous and imported cultures.

Part of Panama's natural beauty and wildlife resides underwater. The name Panama literally translates to "place of abundant fish" and the moniker is no exaggeration. There is certainly a wealth of game fish and the Tropical Star Lodge in Darien Province is considered one of the best places for catching marlin. Do bear in mind, though, that parts of the remote Darien Province are not considered safe for visitors.

For bird watchers, Panama presents a visual feast. The country boasts an incredible diversity of avian life, with species native to both Americas occurring here naturally. There is also an unusually large selection of plant life. There are more than 1,200 species of orchid, over 670 species of fern and more than 1,500 different tree species. Its waters are dotted with 1600 islands, of which Coiba Island is the largest. All in all, it is a great destination for eco-tourism.

Culture

Spanish is the official language of Panama, although there are various other indigenous languages, and English is spoken in certain contexts. Over 75 percent of the population is Roman Catholic. The largest percentage of the population, around 66 percent, is a mixture of European and Native American, with smaller groups of Africans, Europeans, and Native Americans occurring. The culture is Spanish Caribbean in character.

Panama has a population of approximately 3 million people. It is the most industrialized, but least populous nation in Central America. There is a significant community of expat Americans and Europeans, as Panama is regarded as one of the world's top retirement destinations. Despite this, the culture of Panama is loud and vibrant and the country seems to be on a path of speedy growth and development.

There are eight indigenous tribes in Panama. At one time the indigenous people of Panama numbered as many as two million, but today, due to various factors such as warfare and disease, their numbers have dwindled to under 300,000. Two tribes who live mainly on the highlands of Bocas del Toro in Chiriquí Province account for the highest portion of Panama's indigenous people. They are the Ngöbe and the Buglé, who survive by fishing, hunting and animal husbandry, particularly of cattle, pigs, chicken and dogs. Collectively they number close to 180,000 and make up over 60% of Panama's native population. The second largest group is the Kuna, who originated from Columbia and have settled mainly in the Darien Province, on the Caribbean side. Researchers have found that the Kuna have shown a natural resistance against cancer and high blood pressure and also have a strikingly high incidence of albinism. Smaller groups include the Wounaan, the Embera, the Teribe and the Bokota.

Location & Orientation

Panama lies in Central America, between the Caribbean Sea, the Atlantic Ocean and the Pacific Ocean. It occupies a strategic position along the isthmus linking South America to North America. It has almost 2000km of coastline including 1231km on the western (Pacific) side and 685km on the eastern (Caribbean) side. It is bounded by Costa Rica to the north and Colombia to the south. Panama's official currency is the US dollar.

Due to the country's unusual S-shape, you can experience a geographic peculiarity here - observing the sun rising in the Pacific Ocean and setting in the Atlantic. Nowhere else does this occur. At the narrowest point, the landmass separating the Atlantic from the Pacific is only 80km wide. Panama is a popular destination for cruise ships. It is connected to various destinations by air and there are frequent flights between Costa Rica and Panama. The Pan American Highway passes through Panama via Costa Rica, but be aware that its coverage is interrupted at the notorious Darien Gap between Panama and Colombia.

Taxis are plentiful and fairly inexpensive. A ferry service connects Panama City with Isla Contadora in the Pearl Islands. Alternatively, a chartered cruise will enable you to sail through the entire Pearl Islands group. The ferries leave from Naos Island, along Amador Causeway.

Climate & When to Visit

Panama enjoys a tropical maritime climate. As the country is located very close to the equator, temperatures remain consistent throughout the year. Daytime temperatures in Panama City typically settle between 30 and 33 degrees Celsius, with night temperatures dropping to the low 20s. The weather is often humid with a brief dry period occurring between December and April. The lack of rainfall make the months of December, January, February and March the most popular times to visit Panama.

During the rainy months from April to November, mornings can be relatively sunny, with the heaviest downpours occurring in the late afternoon and at night. During these months, the temperatures are slightly cooler.

David is one of the hottest regions, with day averages between 35 and 36.3 degrees Celsius from February to April and between 33 and 34 degrees Celsius during December, January and May. Even from June to November, day temperatures stay above 30 degrees Celsius. Night temperatures stay between 19 and 22 degrees Celsius.

Sightseeing Highlights

Panama City

Panama City is the capital of Panama, with an overall metropolitan population of 1.2 million. It is located at the entrance of the Panama Canal. Although it is a modern city with many skyscrapers, Panama City is surrounded by lush rain forest. As the oldest European settlement in the Americas, the city intrigues with its easy blend of past and future. The abandoned ruins of Panama Viejo offer hints to the lives of the original Spanish colonists, while the Old City, Casco Viejo reflects the colorful melting pot of cultures that is Panama.

Panama Canal

The Panama Canal has been called the 8th wonder. As a triumph of engineering, it remains almost unrivalled. The construction process used 60,000,000 pounds of dynamite and 4 and a half million cubic yards of concrete and it now represents about a third of Panama's total national revenue. Although engineered and planned with US funding, over 90 percent of the labor had been local. The first ship to use the canal was the Ancon, on 15 August 1914.

The Panama Canal consists of a series of six locks, occupying two parallel tracks that either raise or lower the position of the ships. It uses no pumps, but instead relies mainly on the force of gravity. Ships are manoeuvred through the canal by means of a series of "mules", which are attached to the ship with cables. These operate with electricity, which is generated by the canal's own dams. Each lock is just over 300m long. The direction of flow is north to south, rather than east to west.

By using the Panama Canal, a ship en route from New York to San Francisco cuts an incredible 12,700km from the voyage. From 1963, the canal has operated round the clock. The largest number of ships transiting in a single day was 65, and this event occurred on 29 February 1968. Although the canal was opened in 1914, tolls first went up in 1974. Even someone swimming the canal, has to pay a toll, as did Richard Halliburton in 1928. His rate was a mere 36 cents.

Tourists can book a trip on a tour boat (http://www.pmatours.net/pacific_queen/panama_canal_tours/index.html that will pass through the canal system along with the ocean giants. Here you will see the locks and tugboats up close and learn interesting trivia from a knowledgeable guide. There are two options. The partial tour is a one-way trip, north or southbound, that takes approximately 4-5 hours and costs $135. Departure is from Flamenco Marina and includes a full lunch plus beverages. The full tour takes 8-9 hours and includes breakfast, lunch, snacks and refreshments. This experience costs $180 and departure is also from Flamenco Marina.

Miraflores Locks Visitor Center

Canalside, Panama City, Panama
Tel: +507 276-8325

The Panama Canal is an outstanding feat of early 20th century engineering and a visit to the Miraflores Locks Visitors Center should enlighten you on a number of aspects of the project. It includes a four-storey museum that educates on the history of construction and the economics of the Canal through a series of informative displays. This also includes a realistic simulation of ship passing through the Miraflores Locks. Another exhibition focuses on conservation and environmental management.

There are three observation decks, a restaurant and two snack bars. Miraflores is one of two Pacific Locks and the tallest of the three. The system was designed to facilitate passage through the exclusive means of gravity, without any additional use of pumps. The Visitors Center is open from 9am to 5pm, but most activity usually occurs in the afternoon. You could, however, phone ahead for up-to-date information about scheduling. Admission is $8.

Amador Causeway

The Amador Causeway is located at the southern end of the canal and consists of a chain of four islands, constructed to serve as a breakwater to prevent sedimentation in the region of the Port of Balboa. These islands are named Naos, Culebra, Perico and Flamenco. The Causeway was built around the same time as the Canal.

During World War Two, there was a heavy military presence in anticipation of a possible attack on the Panama Canal, particularly on Perico Island, but in recent years, developers have begun to realize the Causeway's potential as tourist spot. It provides great vantage point from which to watch the action in the Canal or for admiring Panama City or the Bridge of the Americas, the connection between the two Americas. The area now has numerous shops and restaurants and you can hire a bicycle to explore at your own pace.

On Naos Island, you will find the Smithsonian Tropical Research Institute, a facility that dates back to 1923 and caters to approximately 900 scientists. A side project of the Smithsonian's work in Panama is the Biodiversity Museum. The building, colorful and eclectic in design, is in itself an attraction. It was conceived by the architect Frank Gehry. Inside, large-scale exhibits illustrate the essential role of Panama's landmass in unifying the biodiversity of North and South. Naos is also a departure point for ferries to the Pearl Islands and Isla Taboga. Flamenco Island, at the other end, has the popular Flamenco shopping center and is also the best place to get a taxi back to Panama City.

Palacio de las Garzas

Palacio de las Garzas or the Herons' Palace is located in Casco Viejo and serves as government offices and residence of the President of Panama. The original building dates back to 1673, and has served as customs house, warehouse, royal winery, residence for the Spanish governor and headquarters for the National Bank. Its name derives from the community of herons that range freely about the grounds. The Tamarind Room, which serves as official dining room, features several murals by the artist, Roberto Lewis. The Yellow Room is used for official events and the Moorish Room dates back to the renovations of 1922.

Panama Viejo

Calle 85 Este and Vía Cincuentenario

Panama Viejo is the location of the original Panama City, which was founded in 1519 by the Spanish Conquistador Pedro Arias Davila. It served as an important base for the conquest of the Inca Empire in Peru and as trading post. When it was destroyed in 1671 by the pirate Henry Morgan, the new city was rebuilt about 8km away. This preserved the layout of the original settlement and provides valuable clues to the structure and community of one of Spain's earliest colonies in the Americas.

The site includes the former convent, a distinctive cathedral tower which dates back to the early 1600s and public buildings centered around the Casas Reales or Royal House. The remains hint at the wealth of Casa Alarcón, the settlement's largest private residence and the Cabildo de la Ciudad, or city hall. Panama Viejo was declared a UNESCO Heritage site in 1996. There is a visitor's center, a museum and a handicraft market. Admission is $6.

Taboga

Isla Taboga or the Island of Taboga is located about an hour away from Panama City by boat trip. The island has an abundance of flowers and pineapples, thanks to its founder, Padre Hernando de Luque, dean of the Cathedral of Panama. The Bishop's Pool, which is at the highest point of the island, was named for Padre Luque, but the island had many other sites linked to the early history of Panama and the Americas.

The settlement on the island dates back to at least1524, and there are still ruins from the time of the Spanish Conquistadors. Its church, Iglesia San Pedro, is the second oldest of the Western Hemisphere. There are conflicting legends regarding the birth of Santa Rosa de Lima, the first saint of the Americas, but some suggest that she was born on Taboga. Another famous person briefly associated with the island, is the Post-Impressionist artist Paul Gauguin, who allegedly lived on the island and worked for a short spell as a laborer on the construction of the Panama Canal.

Three cannons on nearby Isla Morro were used to thwart various attacks, including that of the pirate Captain John Illingworth in 1819 - an event that is also marked by three crosses for three pirate casualties. In 1998, the remains of a possible pirate treasure was uncovered when the building of a new clinic yielded 1000 pieces of silver from the 17th century. Hotel Aspinwall has served several interesting functions, including recuperation center for canal workers and internment camp for German prisoners during World War One.

Lake Gatun

One of the more unique diving locations in Panama is Gatun Lake, which is right beside the Panama Canal. This artificial lake was, at its inception, the largest dam in the world. The region offers opportunities for skiing and boating and provides one of the best sites for freshwater fishing. As the lake has large colonies of peacock bass, there are no restrictions on fishing.

The site includes a fascinating underwater forest, that resulted when the Chagres River was dammed up. Wooded hilltops were transformed into islands and several of these contain a rich diversity of wildlife. Several islands - most notably Islas Tigres (the Tiger Islands) and Islas Las Brujas (the Witch Islands) are considered primate sanctuaries and have populations of spider monkeys, white-faced capuchins and howler monkeys.

Lake Gatun's largest island is Barro Colorado Island, which hosts a bio-diversity study by the Smithsonian Tropical Research Institute. It has 47 snake species, 30 frog species, over 380 bird species, and 480 tree species concentrated on a single land mass. There is a 115 mammal species, which include 75 species of bats alone, as well as sloths, monkeys, agouti, tapirs and coatimundis. It is possible to visit the island for a tour (http://www.stri.si.edu/english/visit_us/barro_colorado/visit.php) that includes a guided trail walk, lunch and a return boat trip. The guided walk typically takes about 3 hours. The visitors center includes a series of informative displays. Admission for the whole tour is $70.

Another popular excursion in this area is Monkey Island (http://monkeyislandpanama.com/), which is accessible by boat trip. A visit could include close encounters with the charming Capuchin monkeys and glimpses at some of the other exotic inhabitants such as toucans, parrots, crocodiles, iguanas, sloths and howler monkeys. Monkey Island lies in the valley of the Chagres River. Bring bug repellent and sun block.

Santa Catalina

It is the tendency of serious surfers to closely guard the secret of a favorite location. The remote fishing village of Santa Catalina is one such hideaway, well known to an inner circle who dedicate their lives to an eternal quest of the perfect wave, but a somewhat enigmatic mystery to most other visitors. In recent years, however, the news of the region's consistent wave action has gotten out and there are now various surf camps that offer accommodation for anything between $5 a night for basic camping to $30 and $40 per night for a room, with meals as an optional extra.

There are various popular surf spots nearby, including Santa Catalina beach, Punta Brava and Punta Roca. Most of these are more suitable to experienced surfers, but El Estero is a little kinder to beginner surfers. San Pedrillo and Cimarron are nearby, but only accessible by boat. Lagartero beach, 10km from Santa Catalina, is popular for swimming, bird watching and horse-riding. Cebaco, the third largest island of Panama, forms part of the nearby Golfo de Montijo Island and is popular for game fishing. Fishing trips can also be arranged with various boat tour operators. There are great scuba diving opportunities about 15 minutes from Playa Santa Catalina, but the region likewise offers easy access to the natural splendor of the Coiba National Park.

The town has a permanent population of about 300 and only one shop, so you will need to stock up on certain essentials such as bug repellent and anti-malaria medication before making your way here. Santa Catalina is accessible only via the slightly larger town of Sona. There is a daily bus service from Sona, which is in turn connected by bus to Panama City.

Coiba Island National Park

http://www.coibanationalpark.com/

Coiba is the largest island in the waters off Panama. Once a notorious prison, especially under the regimes of Omar Torrijos and Manuel Noriega, Coiba Island now serves as a nature reserve, along with a group of over 30 other islands. The prison structures can still be seen on the island.

Coiba Island is mostly covered with virgin rain forest. It offers sanctuary to 97 bird species, including the endangered scarlet macaw and the crested eagle. The island also has a community of howler monkeys and its beaches are home to loggerhead turtles, leatherback turtles, hawksbill turtles and olive turtles. In the nearby waters, you can hope to encounter humpback whales, dolphins, eels, manta rays and spotted rays, jellyfish and barracudas.

Self-powered and silent, kayaks offer a non-invasive mode of exploring the rich marine wildlife of Coiba. To visit the area, you will need a permit from the National Authority for the Environment (Autoridad Nacional del Ambiente or ANAM for short). Snorkelling tours can be organized from nearby Santa Catalina and Coiba Island itself. The region around Coiba boasts a wealth of fishing opportunities - both inshore and offshore - for keen anglers. There are large schools of yellow-fin tuna, black marlin, kubera snapper and roosterfish. To fish in the immediate vicinity of the Coiba Island National Park, a fishing permit of $50 is required per boat. This remains valid for a week. Fishing around Hannibal Bank and Isla Montuosa is unrestricted and needs no permit.

Several walking trails show off the natural splendor of the Coiba Island National Park. The Hot Springs Trail (Sendero Los Pozos Termales) is about 750m long and passes the hot springs, as well as remnants of the prison colony. Some of the wildlife you can hope to encounter here include howler monkeys, plenty of hummingbirds, king vultures and scarlet macaw. Expect to see plenty of monkeys on the appropriately named Monkey's Trail (Sendero de Los Monos). Gambute Peak Trail (Sendero Cerro Gambute) involves some climbing, but will reward you with stunning views. The trail begins at the ANAM Station.

Bocas del Toro

http://www.bocasdeltoro.com/

Bocas del Toro is an archipelago consisting of about 68 tiny islands and keys, located on the Caribbean side of Panama. It is beautifully scenic and offers a wide range of water-based activities for holidaymakers to enjoy. The town, Bocas del Toro is on Isla Colon, which is accessible by boat via Almirante and Changuinola.

Fishing enthusiasts may be interested to know that Bocas del Toro provides ideal conditions for spearfishing. The waters are home to an abundance of grouper, ocean triggerfish, large parrotfish, barracuda and various types of snapper, some weighing up to 18kg. The best time for fishing is when the surf is flat. This occurs between March and May and then again from September to November. The region has tour companies that will equip you with all the right gear, including including fins, mask, snorkel and spear gun. They will also supply the boat.

Bocas del Toro provides several premier surfing spots, particularly on the Islands of Colon Carenero and Bastimentos. Beginners would probably appreciate the swell at Black Rock on Isla Carenero and Wizard Beach on Isla Bastimentos. There is a great beginners beach for all ages on the island, La Feria. Isla Colon offers a greater challenge to more advanced surfers, with Bluff Beach in particular testing the mettle of more experienced surfers with its powerful wave action. Silverbacks on Bastimentos is likewise recommended for experienced surfers. The main surfing season in Panama is from December to March, when waves of 3.5m and higher can be experienced, with a lesser wave swell between 1.2m and 2.4m occurring from May to July.

Since most of the islands are fairly close to each other, Bocas del Toro has various spots that offer calm, sheltered waters and ideal conditions for snorkelling and diving. Admiral Bay has clear water and sheltered coral reefs that drop to 20m. The Isla Bastimentos National Marine Park allows divers the sight of well-preserved reefs and plenty of marine life. Cave diving enthusiasts may wish to explore Cayos Zapatillas. Other favorites are Hospital Point by Isla Solarte and Crawl Key near Isla Cristobel.

Bocas del Toro is less known for its bird watching potential, but Swan Cay is the only place in the Caribbean where the red-billed tropic bird nests. It is also home to various types of gulls, brown pelicans, sandpipers, heron, egret, toucans, parrots, owls, hummingbirds, woodpeckers and tanagers. Various Seagoing turtles, including the loggerhead, leatherback, hawksbill and green turtle have been nesting in Bocas del Toro for hundreds of years. The time to view them is from July through to August and some of the best locations are Bluff Beach on Isla Colon and Long Beach on Isla Bastimentos. There are several communities of Ngobe Indians on Isla Bastimentos. Although there are no formal tours operating in the area, you could inquire with locals about a visit. The Botanical Garden at Isla Colon showcases various native plants and flowers and Butterfly Garden will introduce you to the magical Blue Morpho butterflies.

David

Located in the western part of Panama, David has a population of around 144,800, making it the third largest city in Panama. It is set against the backdrop of the scenic highland regions of the Chiriqui Province, of which it is the capital. As an agricultural center, David is surrounded by plantations of cacao, coffee, sugar and tropical fruit. There are also various cattle ranches. The city serves as a gateway to the flower fields of Boquete and to Cerro Punta. David is about a 45 minute drive away from Paso Canoas, on the border with Costa Rica.

Besides being a holiday destination, David is a popular base for expats, especially from the USA, since its rents are very reasonable. A good place to relax is Parque Cervantes, a great space to indulge in some people watching. There is an attractive fountain, vendors for refreshments and crafters. David was founded in 1602.

Boquete

Although farmers began to settle in the valley towards the end of the 19th century, the town was founded in 1911. The surroundings are mainly rural, with coffee beans being one of the major crops. An important feature is the Caldera River, which runs through Boquete. One of the great attractions of the region is Volcan Baru, the highest peak in Panama. Another popular activity is to take a zip line tour through the Cloud Forest. There are golf courses, and plenty of opportunities for hiking, horseriding, kayaking and white river rafting.

Boquete has an outdoor Tuesday market which sells art, jewellery, homemade wine, organic foods and various crafts. There is a lively art and music scene, which includes the hosting of an annual Jazz Festival. Boquete is a popular place for Americans and Europeans to retire in. Roughly 14 percent of the population is foreign.

Volcan Baru

The best time to visit the summit of Volcan Baru, Panama's only volcano and highest peak, is at daybreak. On a clear day, it may be possible to see both the Pacific and Atlantic Oceans. Volcan Baru is 3,478m high and is located within the Talamanca mountain range, about 35km from the Costa Rican border. The peak is a remnant of a far larger stratovolcano, and it is estimated that its most recent eruption may have occurred in the 16th century.

Volcan Baru can be reached by means of a hiking trail or by a 4x4 track. The hiking route is clearly marked. Many hikers elect to begin their excursion around midnight, which should see them at the top of the summit when sunrise occurs. Another strategy is to take two days and spend the first night at the Fogones campground which offers some form of shelter. Jeep tours are available. Dress warmly as early morning temperatures at the top of Volcan Baru can be rather chilly.

Pearl Islands

The Pearl Islands lie scattered across the Gulf of Panama, like a giant jigsaw with over 200 separate pieces. The largest of the group is Isla del Rey or "Island of the King", which is, after Coiba, the biggest island belonging to Panama. It boasts four towns and a population of around 1,670 people. Other islands include Contadora, a popular resort island where the last Shah of Iran spent a brief period of his exile and Mogo Mogo, a setting for one season of the reality TV series Survivor. The Pearl Islands were also used for another recent television production, The Real Swiss Family Robinson. While the Survivor battles were mainly staged and supervised, the tranquil Pearl Islands had been the unfortunate setting for far bloodier power struggles in the distant past, with the Spanish decimating the original inhabitants of the region in large numbers, to claim the lucrative pearl harvest exclusively for themselves.

A totally different bounty that the Pearl Islands offer visitors today, is that of its beauty and its marine wildlife. The islands are great for bird watching and between August and December, whales visit the region. The Pearl Islands are equally popular for diving (http://www.coral-dreams.com/) and snorkelling, as there are various interesting rock formations and different types of coral such as orange and brain coral. A wealth of marine species call these waters home. They include butterfish, angelfish, sandfish, parrotfish, eels, brown shark, reef shark, sting ray, manta ray and lobster.

San Blas Islands

Located in the Caribbean, on the eastern side of Panama, the San Blas Islands are the ancestral lands of the Kuna Yala tribe, who maintain the lifestyle of centuries past. Although many of their dugout canoes are now motorized, they still subsist mainly by fishing and gathering fruit and wear the beads and mola garments of their culture. Coconut palms are abundant and, until recent times, the coconut was a form of currency on the islands.

The surroundings are rich in coral reefs and some of the islands themselves are also of coral. The region is semi-autonomous and a great place to learn more about Kuna culture. The waters are good for snorkelling and sport fishing. As English is rarely spoken, you may need to familiarize yourself with a few basic phrases of Spanish. There are daily flights between Panama City and El Porvenir, the capital of the region. Another great way to explore the San Blas Islands, is through a boat cruise (http://sailingsanblasislands.com/). In total, there are over 370 islands of varying size.

Recommendations for the Budget Traveler

Places to Stay

Central Park Hotel

Calle Miguel Brostella, El Dorado, Panama City, Panama
http://www.centralparkpanama.com/index-en.php

Central Park Hotel is located within a 5 minute stroll of El Dorado.

It has a spa, casino, restaurant, lobby bar, swimming pool and offers a shuttle service. Rooms include a well-equipped kitchenette with microwave, fridge and coffee-maker, a safe box, television and hairdryer. The hotel is wheelchair friendly and offers free parking and free high-speed internet. Accommodation begins at $61 and includes breakfast.

Metro Hotel Panama

Calle D El Cangrejo, Panama City, Panama
Tel: 507 202-5050
http://www.metrohotelpanama.com/

The Metro Hotel Panama is located conveniently near the casinos, night clubs, shops and restaurants. The hotel is wheelchair friendly and staff are helpful. Rooms are comfortable and include such conveniences as a fridge, safe, iron, coffeemaker and LCD TV. Free parking and free high-speed internet is available. Accommodation begins at $90 and includes a continental breakfast.

Hotel Residencial Cervantes

Avenida 2a Este David 507, Panama
Tel: +507 777 1055

The Hotel Residencial Cervantes is located within 5 minutes walk from the city center, 100m from a casino and 2 minutes from Parque Cervantes.

It is a small hotel and rooms are basic, but spacious, clean and well maintained, with air-conditioning and bathroom amenities. Each room has a television and free parking is available. Reception is available round the clock. The hotel also offers free coffee and free high-speed internet. Accommodation begins at $39 per night.

Hotel Refugio de Montana

Santa Lucia, Boquete 507, Panama
Tel: +507 730-8355
http://refugiodemontana.com/

Hotel Refugio de Montana is located in a tranquil environment just a short drive from Boquete. There is a back garden with fruit trees and outdoor seating and the interiors are equally charming. Rooms include cable TV, private and modern bathroom facilities and free Wi-Fi coverage. Free parking is available and a light continental breakfast is served. Accommodation is charged at between $44 and $50 per night for two persons. An additional 11 percent tax is levied.

Hotel Hibiscusgarden

Playa Lagartero, Lagartero, Panama
http://www.hibiscusgarden.com/

The Hibiscus Garden Hotel is a small establishment located on Lagartero beach, which is about 10 minutes drive from Santa Catalina. Rooms are basic, but functional and the decor incorporates natural elements such as driftwood and seashells. Various activities such as horseriding, wakeboarding and scuba diving can be arranged through the hotel and there is a shuttle service available to Santa Catalina, although this may be charged for. The hotel also has a restaurant. There are several accommodation options. The advanced dorm costs $15 per person, or $25 for single occupancy. The family rooms sleep two for $55 and include a bathroom and private terrace. The unspoilt remoteness of the location does mean that Internet access may be weak or non-existent.

Places to Eat & Drink

Lenos & Carbon

Isla Flamenco, Panama City, Panama
Tel: +507 314 1650

Lenos & Carbon have various outlets around Panama City. The one on the Amador Causeway offers a great view of the marina, but can be super busy, due to its popular location. There is another outlet at Albrook Mall. One of the house specialities is a mixed grill that combines beef steak, pork ribs and chicken breast, which is served with rice, salad and fries and costs just $13. Other dishes include grilled chicken salad, coconut shrimp, fillet mignon and grilled salmon. Beverages include margaritas, mojitos, milkshakes and many more.

Tinajas

Bella Vista, Calle 51, Panama City, Panama
Tel: +507 263 7890
http://www.tinajaspanama.com/

Visit Tinajas, if you want to experience a multi-faceted taste of authentic Panamanian entertainment. The decor includes traditional motifs and from 9pm, you will be treated to a show featuring Panamanian folk dancing.

The food is affordable and includes fried squid, chicken breast in orange sauce, mixed kebab with beef, chicken and shrimp, Yucca country pie, seafood casserole and the ever-popular corvina. Besides a few of the usual standards, dessert options include seasonal tropical fruit and home made coconut custard.

PaParrillada Jimmy

Via Cincuentenaria, Near ATLAPA, Panama City, Panama
http://www.parrilladajimmy.com/

Jimmy's has an extensive menu that includes a variety of pasta dishes, salads, pizzas, red meat options, chicken, sandwiches, seafood and desserts. Corvina, which is a local favorite similar to sea bass, is prepared in several different ways, including grilled, breaded, as fish fingers and in kebabs. Other seafood choices include monkfish, squid, red snapper and shrimp. Other mains include lamb chops, pork chops, T-bone steak, sheesh kebab and mousaka. There is a large selection of starters and a wide choice in wines. Prices range from pita breads and soups for between $2 and $3, to pastas between $6 and $10, to generous, meaty mains of up to $20.

Big Daddy's Grill, Boquete

Downtown Main Street, 1 block South of Park
Across from Explora Ya & Casa Solution, Boquete 0413, Panama
Tel: +507 6683 3354
https://www.facebook.com/BigDaddysGrillBoquete

Big Daddy's Grill is centrally located and offers a combination of funky indoor and outdoor seating. A mainstay of the menu is fresh fish, which is prepared in various ways, but a signature dish is the fish tacos. You can also order vegetarian tacos, shrimp tacos, chicken tacos and more. Other favorites include corn dogs, New England chowder, and fillet mignon. There are several salad, sandwich and burger options, including the vegan burgers and some of the dessert choices are home made ice cream, lemon tart and apple tart. Big Daddy's Grill serves excellent margaritas. Fresh ingredients are used. Expect to pay somewhere between $3 and $12.

Super Gourmet Bocas

3rd Street (Main Street), Bocas Town, Isla Colon 10700, Panama
Tel: +507 757 9357
http://supergourmetbocas.com/

Super Gourmet is deli and shop in Bocas town which offers a large selection of local produce to enjoy on the premises or as take-aways. The shop caters for a huge variety of tastes and dietary requirements.

There is, for example, a large kosher section, as well as a full range of products that are vegetarian, gluten-free, sugar-free or lactose free. You can purchase sandwiches made to order, muffins, quiche, vegetarian lasagne, pizza bread, curry devil eggs, brownies and more. You can choose from various salads such as seaweed salad, chicken salad, Greek salad, potato salad and coleslaw, as well as a number of cold meats such as pastrami, smoked turkey, chorizo, roast beef and salami. The chocolate is organically made and sold in several combinations. The shop is a must for foodies. There is also a Super Gourmet outlet at Avenida A y Calle 6 in Casco Viejo, Panama City.

Places to Shop

Mola & other Kuna Handicrafts

Kuna Co-operative
Avenida Arnulfo Arias Madrid, Panama City

The Kuna are one of the larger indigenous groupings in Panama and the colorful mola they create (these are applique and reversed applique panels) make popular keepsakes and souvenirs. Mola are used to make traditional blouses, but can also be combined with beach bags and cushions. A mola blouse is referred to as a tulemola or dulemola. The Kuna have a strong tradition for trading in craft items, that goes back centuries, and many of the handicraft items are sold through family businesses.

A great place to browse for traditional handicrafts made by Kuna women is the Kuna Co-operative, a market that trades on Avenida Arnulfo Arias Madrid in Panama City. Popular items are the bead bands that the Kuna themselves wear around their arms and legs.

Reprosa

corner of Samuel Lewis Ave & 54th Street (Next to Plaza Obario), Panama City
Tel: 507 269 0457
http://www.reprosa.com/

The indigenous art treasures of Panama fascinate through their elegant design and their rarity. At Reprosa, you can admire a beautiful collection of jewellery based on Spanish Colonial and Pre-Colombian designs. A tour provides some insight into workshop techniques. The shop also sells a variety of other craft items such as Embera baskets, Kuna mola panels, and carvings, as well as Panama hats. Most of the items are either made by Reprosa or local artisans. Jewellery pieces are priced at between $18 and $300, and crafted from silver or gold. The business is family owned.

Crafts in Panama

A shop that offers the largest collection of mola work is Flory Saltzman Molas, located on Vía Veneto, near the entrance to Hotel El Panamá El Cangrejo in Panama City. Prices vary and the ones with the most intricate detail may cost more than the wares of informal vendors.

Helene Breebaart incorporates mola appliqué to create unique designer wear. She trades at Calle 50 and Calle 39, but specializes in customized garments. The Casco Antiguo Flea market trades on Sundays at Plaza Cathedral de San Felipe. Besides craft items, you can also buy second hand fashion clothing, antiques, books and music. A YMCA handicrafts market trades at the corner of Avenida Arnulfo Arias Madrid and Amador in Balboa, selling mainly traditional Kuna and Emberá arts and crafts. There is a large market, the Mercado Nacional de Artesanías in Panama Viejo, right next to the Visitor Center.

Flamenco Shopping Plaza

Amador Causeway, Isla Flamenco, Panama City
Tel: 507-314-0932

The Flamenco Shopping Center may easily see to all of your shopping requirements. It is located along the attractive Amador Causeway and some of the goods sold in its shops include cigars, jewellery, souvenirs, leatherwork and other traditional handicraft items. The Flamenco Shopping Center also has duty-free shops, where you may be able to buy some real bargains.

Karavan Gallery

Calle 3, between Avenida A & Central | Casco Viejo, Panama City, Panama
Tel: +507 228-5161
http://www.karavan-gallery.com/

Located in the Casco Viejo part of Panama City, Karavan Gallery sells handicraft items from the Kuna, Embera, Waunaan and Sofre communities. A wide selection of art and craft is showcased here. There are interesting and innovative designs featuring Kuna textiles and some of the other goods include baskets, masks, paintings, vases, pillowcases, tablecloths and ceremonial hats.

Costa Rica

Costa Rica is sometimes referred to as "the Switzerland of Central America." And no wonder...the comfortable lifestyle, peaceful government, and stunning natural wonders make this small Central American country the perfect vacation spot.

Whether you prefer hiking on pristine rainforest trails among howler monkeys and toucans, or sipping margaritas on the Caribbean Coast, Costa Rica has something for everyone.

History buffs will thrill at the ruins of 3000-year-old Guayabo de Turrialba, as well as the pre-Columbian architecture found in cities throughout the country. If city-life is more your style, the bustling capital of San Jose is home to six major museums, a handful of stunning parks and plazas, open-air markets, and restaurants and bars galore.

If you're interested in hiking, Costa Rica's 35 national parks cover 11% of the country, and boast hiking trails for all levels. (If you're up to the 2-day climb of Cerro Chirripo, a hike to the 3820m peak yields a view that spreads from the Pacific to the Caribbean Ocean.)

Culture

For the people of Costa Rica, the frequent reply of "pura vida" ("pure life") to the question "How are you?" isn't just a slang term…it's a way of life. It symbolizes the Costa Rican ideal of sitting back and enjoying the beauty of life. Costa Ricans pride themselves on being friendly, helpful, and easygoing. Family is important to Costa Ricans, and many live in extended family units. In 2012, Costa Rica was ranked number one in the Happy Planet Index, a rating based on life expectancy, ecological footprint, and subjective life satisfaction.

The people of Costa Rica are 75% Catholic, and Spanish is the national language. Costa Ricans have managed to maintain a country of peace and relative prosperity, despite the conflict that occasionally rages in nearby countries. In the absence of war, Costa Rica boasts the highest standard of living in Central America.

Primary education is free and compulsory for school-aged children, and for the large part, Costa Rican youth have ample time to worry about dating, music, fashion, and of course, soccer. Tourism is a major source of Costa Rica's income, and the people of Costa Rica have certainly made their country worth touring.

Costa Rica's popular proverb panza llena, corazon contento ("full stomach, happy heart") sums up the nation's love of savory dishes, preferably eaten with good company. Costa Rican cuisine leans more toward the mild blends of garlic and herbs than spicy chili peppers or piquant powders. The unofficial national dish of gallo pinto — black beans and rice, seasoned with onion, sweet pepper, cilanthro and Lizano sauce — will satisfy all palates.

Visitors to Costa Rica can also enjoy fried plantains, tamales, and empanadas. Refreshing natural fruit juices grace the tables of both 5-star restaurants and "sodas" (small restaurants that serve affordable and healthy local fare). And of course, you can't leave the country without a taste of the nation's most famous commodity…its rich and flavorful coffee.

Location & Orientation

Nestled between Nicaragua and Panama, Costa Rica is a small Central American country with the Pacific Ocean on one side and the sparkling Caribbean on the other. Located within the Northwestern hemisphere, Costa Rica is near the equator, between latitudes 8° and 12°N, and longitudes 82° and 86°W. It is roughly 1170 km (730 miles) to the southwest of Jamaica, Haiti, and the Cayman islands.

With five major mountain ranges, fourteen river systems, and four volcanoes (two of them active) within its 51,000 sq km, Costa Rica is home to startlingly diverse ecosystems, and is considered one of the most biologically diverse areas of the planet.

It's no wonder that with so many natural resources, Costa Rica is making efforts to protect and sustain the land. Costa Rica is known as one of the "greenest" countries on the planet, being the only one to successfully meet all five criteria set forth by the United Nations Development Programme for environmental sustainability in 2011. They are currently working towards becoming the first carbon-neutral country by the year 2021.

Climate & When to Visit

Even though Costa Rica is slightly smaller than the U.S. state of Virginia, the weather varies enormously because of the country's geographical diversity. The highlands stay fairly cold and the cloud forests remain misty and cool. The Pacific and Caribbean coasts are hot year-round, and the Central Valley experiences an "eternal spring." Travelers to Costa Rica should pack for this variance in temperatures, preparing for humidity and rain as well as brilliant sunshine.

Costa Rica's main weather consists of a "dry season" and a "wet season," although it rains frequently year-round. The dry season, or "summer," lasts from December through April, with local schools closing from December to February for "summer vacation." May begins the rainy season, which lasts until December. The average temperature throughout the year is between 22 to 27 degrees Celsius (71 and 81 degrees Fahrenheit).

For those wishing to avoid the tourist bustle and save some money, the best time to travel to Costa Rica is May. Lodging is cheaper, and attractions won't be as crowded. You will need an umbrella, however, and be prepared to deal with a few muddy roads.

Costa Rica has two main tourist seasons. Prices may be higher and crowds thicker during these months. Costa Rica is busy from December to April, and, because of a high number of North American and European tourists, in June and July. If you are planning on traveling during these months, be sure to plan well in advance.

You may also wish to plan your vacation around your interests...surfers may seek out the high and fast waves from late June to September on the Pacific coast and from November to May on the Caribbean coast. Turtle season is a popular and stunning time to visit the Caribbean side of Costa Rica, lasting from late February to October. Bird enthusiasts will find stunning birds year-round, but for those seeking the resplendent quetzal, November through April are the best months to plan your trip.

Sightseeing Highlights

Canopy & Zip-line Tours

A trip to Costa Rica is incomplete without a canopy tour. Most tours consist of zip-lines through the rainforest, but some include aerial trams, suspension bridges, and lookout towers. Zip-line canopy tours are by far the most popular. Visitors climb to a starting platform high in the canopy, and then don a harness that can be attached to cables strung between trees. One deep breath, and then you're flying through the air, taking in the sights and sounds around you as you zoom from one platform to another.

Canopy tours provide a unique perspective of the flora and fauna of the ecosystem. You may catch a glimpse of toucans, monkeys, and sloths as you zoom from platform to platform, or glide tranquilly on an aerial tram. Depending on the area you're in, panoramic views of mountain ranges, volcanoes, and oceans can complete the perfection of the experience. Canopy tours are available in almost every tourist destination.

The most highly recommended canopy tour companies in Costa Rica are the Original Canopy Tour company, which provides tours in Drake Bay, Monteverde, Mahogany Park, and Limon; Adventura Canopy Tours in Monteverde; Dream Forest Canopy Tour in Manuel Antonio; and Poas Canopy Tour outside of San Jose. If you're not in any of these areas, check with your lodging for a good nearby canopy tour.

Visitors should expect to pay between $30 and $80 for a canopy tour. Many companies offer student and child discounts. Look for companies that provide meals and transportation to and from tour locations to get the most out of your money. It is also customary to tip your guides, so be sure to bring some extra cash. Most tours last 2 to 3 hours, and require a liability form to be signed. If you are traveling with small children, be sure to check if the canopy tour has an age limit.

Also, rememeber to bring plenty of sunscreen and bug spray. Tennis shoes are also preferred to sandals, in part because of the climbing usually involved in reaching platforms, but also because you might lose a shoe to the forest floor as you're zipping through the air!

Coffee & Chocolate Tours

Costa Rica's rich volcanic soil and temperate climate make it an ideal growing place for coffee beans and cacao. Visitors with a culinary bent will love the opportunity to discover the processes that bring coffee to their cups and chocolate to their plates. Whether you're interested in touring a small family-run organic farm or a large plantation, Costa Rica won't disappoint.

Costa Rican coffee blends are famous the world over. Farmers first began cultivating coffee in 1798, and soon it was so successful that it surpassed the production of cacao (chocolate) and tobacco. A coffee tour allows visitors to witness a coffee bean's humble journey from seed to cup.

At some farms, visitors are even permitted to pick coffee fruits during harvest season from November to March. After the harvest, visitors learn how the coffee is removed from the husk at the processing plant. Then they move on to discover the drying process and view the roasting mill before enjoying a fresh cup of rich coffee at the end.

Café Britt near Heredia offers two tours: the Classic Coffee Tour and the Coffee Lovers' Tour, which incorporates humor, theatre, and historical facts. Coopedota in Santa Maria de Dota is made up of 800 local coffee farmers, and is especially popular from November to March, when guests are invited to join the harvest.

Doka Estate is an award-winning coffee-producer on the slopes of Poas Volcano, and the 100-year-old plantation uses a traditional water mill to power their processing plant. Espiritu Santo in Naranjo boasts 640 acres of coffee fields, and for an extra fee, guests can take lessons from an expert taster on the finer points of coffee roasts. Monteverde's coffee mill is also used to peel cherries and sun-dry beans, and the tour of their facility is one of the best in the area.

If you prefer the sweetness of chocolate to the richness of coffee, there are also a handful of cacao farmers that offer tours. Chocolate has been made in Costa Rica for thousands of years, and the unique flavor of Latin American chocolate makes a chocolate tour a culinary delight. Learn how cacao is harvested and processed, and of course, sample various chocolates as you go.

Most chocolate farms are located on the outskirts of Puerto Viejo. To get a taste of the traditional chocolate-making process of the Mayans, make a reservation to tour the ChocRart organic cacao farm in Playa Chiquita. Other chocolate tours are available at the Bribri Indigenous Reserve, the Tirimbina Rainforest Center, at the family-run La Iguana Chocolate Farm, and at Finca Kobo.

Both chocolate tours and coffee tours are usually between $15 and $40, and run in the mornings and afternoons. Some tours aren't available year-round, so be sure to check tour schedules before making plans.

Beaches

With nearly 1300 km of coastline, Costa Rica boasts some of the most beautiful beaches in the world. From Playa Tamarindo, with it's shopping and dining amusements, to Manuel Antonio's perfect horseshoe bays, travelers will love the sand between their toes and the water that stays warm year-round. It's hard to find a beach you won't enjoy, but choosing the best beach to visit all depends on the kind of experience you're looking for.

If you're looking for secluded beaches for sunbathing and swimming, the Osa peninsula on the Pacific coast is lined with beaches that are usually un-crowded and idyllic. Montezuma has a few more shops, but its Bohemian atmosphere will put you under a spell of sea, sand, and sun.

Shops and restaurants along some beaches offer visitors to Costa Rica more excitement, if you care to dance the night away or buy lunch on the beach. Paseo de los Turistas in Puntarenas or Playa Tamarindo are great places to wander the shops and enjoy delectable local fare in between swimming and sunning on the sand.

Surfers will find some of the best surfing available on the beaches of Costa Rica. Playa Hermosa is one of the few beaches in the world that provides lights for night-surfing. Surfers also flock to Playa Pavones, Santa Teresa, Avellanas, and north Guiones. The highest waves can be ridden from late June to September on the Pacific coast and from November to May on the Caribbean coast.

Research the best beaches in the areas you'll be visiting. Some beaches offer snorkeling, surfboard rentals, horseback riding, and wildlife excursions. Others boast casinos and nightclubs. But whatever your interests, remember that because Costa Rica is so close to the equator, visitors should make sure to use a good sunscreen, even on cloudy days. Aside from being a health risk, a bad sunburn can ruin the rest of your trip.

Beach-goers may find carrying cash more convenient at the less crowded beaches, as ATMs may be harder to find, and not every vendor accepts cards.

Arenal Volcano

Arenal is considered the third-most perfect volcanic cone in the world, and it's one of the ten most active volcanoes in the world. It's a popular attraction, and for good reason. On clear nights, travelers can watch the spectacular lava flows, whether from their hotel, or while soaking in one of the many naturally-heated hot springs nearby. In fact, Tabacon Hot Springs is one of the most beautiful in the world, set among lush greenery, clear waterfalls and rare orchids. The Arenal area boasts a number of resorts and day spas, if you're looking for a unique way to relax in a stunning environment.

If you prefer something a bit more thrilling, you can go whitewater rafting or try your hand at the exciting sport of waterfall repelling. Hikes are also available through the surrounding forest and over suspension bridges, and local guides provide information about the flora and fauna visitors are sure to encounter. Horseback rides are also available, as well as fishing, kayaking, and boat tours. Be sure to visit the La Catarata de la Fortuna, a beautiful 70m waterfall that will take your breath away.

La Fortuna de San Carlos is the charming town located at the foot of the volcano, with plenty of accommodations for travelers of every budget. The hotels in the main plaza area have some of the best views of the volcano. Many hotels also offer deals on spa services and tours. Be sure to check what your hotel offers.

And don't worry too much about the volcano having a major eruption while you're in the area. The last large eruption took place in 1968, and the volcano has spent the years since then continually "letting off steam," releasing the seismic tension through a mellow ongoing eruption. Things have been pretty quiet since October 2010, but despite this, geologists warn visitors to stick to the trails and not explore restricted areas. Instability in spots near the volcano can make exploring dangerous, and leaving the prescribed paths is prohibited. You can learn more about the volcano's geological history and recent activity by visiting www.arenal.net.

If you're determined to view the lava flows, you may need to stay in the area for up to a week, since cloud cover is unpredictable, especially during the rainy months between May and November. But with no shortage of activities, a week may not be long enough for visitors to get their fill!

Tortuguero Turtle Nesting Area

The nesting of sea turtles is one of the nature's most amazing spectacles, and Tortuguero Beach is one of the most important nesting sites of the endangered green turtle in the Northern Hemisphere. On January nights, the beaches swarm with Leatherback Sea Turtles, and the tiny hatchlings rushing to sea is a truly magnificent sight. Local guides are trained to give tours during the various nesting seasons of green, Leatherback, hawksbill, and loggerhead turtles.

The green turtle is still nearing extinction, despite Tortuguero becoming a protected site in 1959. Unfortunately, the turtles and their eggs continue to be illegally harvested for bars and restaurants in Limon and San Jose. You can help prevent the sea turtles' continued endangerment by avoiding restaurants and bars that serve turtle eggs and meat.

Currently, only 1 in 5000 turtles will survive to adulthood. Because of this devastating statistic, both nesting mothers and baby turtles should not be disturbed by flashlights or flash photography, and should not be touched. The nesting and hatching of turtles is a stunning sight that should be viewed from a short distance away, giving mother and baby turtles space enough to safely make their way to the shore and back to the ocean.

In addition to the exciting spectacle of nesting turtles, scenic boat and kayak excursions through the lush jungle are also available in Tortuguero. Scenic boat tours are especially popular, with local guides pointing out the abundant wildlife, including various birds, monkeys, and butterflies.

Visitors are encouraged to hire local guides in Tortuguero, rather than hiring guides in San Jose, since the local economy depends on tourism. Aside from helping boost a local economy, you'll have a more authentic experience.

Because of its remote location, Tortuguero has no roads leading to the village, and is accessible only by boat or plane. Travelers should be sure to bring cash to Tortuguero…there are no banks or ATMs in the city, and credit cards are only accepted in a few locations.

Monteverde Cloud Forest

Whether you're a nature-lover or not, you'll be astounded at the flora and fauna that fills this beautiful reserve. Monteverde is considered a "biological hotspot" due to the diversity of life it harbors. Because it covers six distinct biological zones, it is home to more than 2,000 species of plants and trees, 100 species of mammals, over 400 species of birds, and roughly 1,200 species of amphibians and reptiles. Multiple hikes are available for varying levels of ability, as well as canopy tours for those who'd like a bird's eye view of the forest. Horseback rides are also a beautiful and relaxing way to take in the scenery.

The area also has a wonderful selection of natural museums to explore. Check out the creepy crawlies of the cloud forest at the World of Insects ("Mundo de los Insectos"), watch over 40 species of snakes slither at Serpentario, or take a look at some of the 20 species of frogs and toads at Ranario. If you're traveling with children, these museums are a fun and interactive way to learn more about the ecology of the area, while providing a pleasant break from hiking or other activities.

Another unique attraction of Monteverde is the twilight and night-time guided tours of various paths through the forest. Equipped with a flashlight, visitors can catch a glimpse of various nocturnal creatures just beginning to wake up. For the perfect evening, hike a trail that allows you to watch the sunset before making your way back down in time to catch a night hike.

To truly experience all Monteverde has to offer, travelers are encouraged to spend at least three days exploring local sights. Accommodations are available in any of the small nearby towns of Santa Elena, Cerro Plano, and the Quaker-founded Monteverde itself. Be sure to dress in layers and bring an umbrella…Monteverde's climate is colder and wetter than other areas of Costa Rica. If you're planning on hiking, be sure to make a stop at the entrance beforehand; there are no restrooms on the trails.

Cerro Chiripo

This strenuous climb is not for the faint of heart, but for those up to the challenge, the 2-day trek allows hikers to experience seven distinct ecosystems on their way to the 3820m peak. 18 km (11 miles) and 3,000 meters of elevation gain (10,000 feet) make this hike a challenging one. But those who succeed are afforded stunning views. On a clear day, both the Pacific and the Caribbean are visible from the top of the mountain.

Those wishing to scale the mountain should be sure to prepare well: sunscreen, plenty of water with a system for purifying more, and a good sleeping bag are absolute necessities. There are two main areas to camp about halfway up the mountain, so you don't need to carry a tent, although you will need a cook stove and your own water. Be sure to go heavy on the sunscreen! Between the elevation and the location near the equator, you can be so badly sunburned that you can be hospitalized.

You will need to make a reservation through the park system to climb Cerro Chiripo. Visitors should go to the ranger station and make a reservation in person. If you call, you may be told there is a long waiting list.

If you make the climb, prepare to be amazed by the wildlife you encounter. Starting in stunning forests, climbers will make their way through pastures to a tundra ecosystem that keep biologists fascinated for years. Above the pastures and tundra, hikers will enter tropical evergreen forest and then move upwards into the rainforests where they'll find oak trees that tower at 50 meters (165 feet) or higher, with bamboo and ferns surrounding them on the ground.

As hikers climb higher, vegetation lays lower to the ground, and by the time climbers reach the harsh atmosphere at the top of the mountain, they may wonder if they're somewhere in the southwestern United States!

If you'd prefer to remain closer to sea level, there are other trails to hike as well, and you won't be disappointed by the respite from the heat and humidity of the rainforest. There is a natural hot spring about 15 minutes north of the ranger station in San Ferardo de Rivas, and, a short ways to the south, the Wilson Botanical Gardens near San Vito will take your breath away.

Whitewater Rafting

The stunning rivers of Costa Rica attract thousands of river runners each year. Thrill-seekers will get their adrenaline fix during the rainy months of June through October, when the rivers are high and wild. Beginning rafters can enjoy calmer waters from November to April.

In the Central Pacific, river runners can book a variety of trips ranging from half-day to multi-week length adventures. Class II to IV rapids make this a thrilling area to raft.

If you're in the Arenal Volcano area, check out two of Costa Rica's favorite whitewater rafting destinations. The Class III Balsa River and the Class IV Toro river will give a heart-pounding adventure experience. If you'd prefer something calmer, the Penas Blancas River, 20 minutes away, is a well-known destination for safari floats.

Near San Jose, experienced guides run rafting trips down the Pacuare and Reventazon rivers. Scenic waters course through a steep gorge with stunning views. Package trips purchased in San Jose often include transportation, food, and river guides to help rafters negotiate Class II and Class V rapids.

Tubing adventures in the North Pacific include a short horseback ride through tropical dry forest, before floating down Rio Negro among mild Class I and II rapids, making this trip one of the most enjoyable tubing excursions in the country.

The Caribbean coast offers tranquil safari floats in addition to Class II to Class IV rapids. If you're in the Southern Caribbean, be sure to float the Estrella River through banana plantations and the Cabecar Indiginous Reserve before suiting up for the rapids.

Museums of San Jose

Whether you're interested in contemporary art by Latin American artists, archeological artifacts of gold and jade, or geographical and scientific exhibits, San Jose's six major museums have something for everyone. Many museums offer student discounts, as well.

The Museum of Costa Rican Art is housed in the terminal of the old airport, making the art deco building a work of art in itself. 3,200 pieces call the museum home, while traveling exhibits fill remaining galleries. Be sure to visit the sculpture garden as well. Entrance costs $5, with a student price of $3.

The Jade Museum is located in the largest building in Central America, and holds the world's largest collection of Pre-Columbian jade. Pieces date from 500 B.C. to 800 A.D., and recent renovations to the lighting show each spectacular shade of green in ways that will take your breath away. Admission is $2.

The National Gallery of Contemporary Art and Design emphasizes current trends in Latin American art and design. The gallery utilizes a spectacular maze of theatres, libraries and galleries on Avenida 3 to showcase modern art. Admission is 600 colones.

All that glitters is gold at the Gold Museum, where the processes and uses of Pre-Columbian gold are displayed. Hundreds of pieces explain gold's place in indigenous cultures, and the museum also houses a special exhibit of rare coins and bills. Entrance costs $6, with a student price of $3.

The National Museum is small, but offers a fascinating glimpse into Costa Rica's history, from Pre-Columbian indigenous culture through colonial life up to the present day. The Old Fort building of the museum still has bullet holes from the 1948 revolution. Admission is $4, with a $2 price for students.

The Children's Museum is a great attraction for those traveling with young children. Hands-on exhibits illustrate concepts from science and technology to culture and literature, including a fun house and an earthquake simulator. Because the building used to be a jail, there is even an exhibit about what life was like for the prisoners! Admission is 800 colones for adults and 500 colones for children.

Puerto Viejo de Talamanca

Located in the Limon province, the city is a blend of perfect beaches, spectacular surfing, and a swinging night life. Though more "touristy" than the rest of Costa Rica, it's worth visiting to dance to the local reggae music and to watch surfers ride some of the best waves in the world…or even tackle some yourself!

While this was once a small fishing town, it has grown into a party city popular with the young and hip. Accommodations are reasonably priced, and shopping opportunities abound. The area is the perfect combination of Caribbean flavor and laid-back attitude.

The Afro-Caribbean presence is strong, and reggae music permeates the streets. But reggae isn't the only sound…music-lovers will find everything from salsa to hip-hop to rock and roll being played on the radio and in local nightclubs. The cuisine of local restaurants is equally varied. Dishes are influenced by Mexico, Italy, China, and the Caribbean islands.

A variety of nightclubs, discos, restaurants and casinos make Puerto Viejo a night time hotspot, and visitors will find plenty of places to dance the night away, or to just sit back and enjoy the atmosphere.

Though the surfing is good, strong rip currents make swimming at Puerto Viejo's beaches unadvisable. Travelers should also know that most of the streets are unpaved and in poor condition, so driving is unadvisable as well. However, the dirt roads add a rustic feel to the town, and walking is an enjoyable way to see the sights.

PANAMA & COSTA RICA TRAVEL GUIDE

Recommendations for the Budget Traveler

Places to Stay

Because one of Costa Rica's main industries is tourism, you're likely to find reasonable accommodations wherever you travel.

Hostels are even available for those on a shoestring budget, but for the most part, clean and friendly hotels are available for those not wishing to break the bank with their accommodation costs. Here are a few highly recommended accommodations in several areas throughout Costa Rica.

Tree Houses Hotel near Arenal

300 Meters Norte de Cementario de la Florencia
Santa Clara, San Carlos, Costa Rica
011 (506) 2475-6507
http://treehouseshotelcostarica.com/
$95 - $140/night

This isn't the cheapest hotel in Arenal, but tree houses set in the jungle make this hotel a unique and memorable part of your Costa Rica stay, and the hotel has received several awards for service.

The staff is personable and friendly, and visitors report feeling welcome. Services include a free night hike, $8 laundry service, and transportation. There is also a hotel spa that offers massages and facials ranging from $20 - $55. The tree houses offer the best views of wildlife, and monkeys and sloths make frequent appearances. This hotel is located near a busy roadway, however, so it may not be an ideal stay if you're a light sleeper. But if you don't mind the gentle hum of the occasional car going by, this hotel is unlike anything else you'll find the world over.

Casa Batsu in the Monteverde Cloud Forest

located next to the Monteverde Welcome Center
Monteverde Cloud Forest Reserve, Costa Rica
(506) 245-5572
http://www.casabatsu.org/
$75 - $264/night

This Bed & Breakfast is an ideal location for those wishing to explore the Monteverde area, and the owners are known for their hospitality and friendliness. A large garden provides the perfect place to relax, and rooms are available with or without kitchenettes. The staff is extremely knowledgeable about local restaurants, tours, and excursions. Visitors feel like honored guests, and it's a perfect place to stay if traveling with family. One of the strongest selling points of this hotel is its proximity to the Monteverde Welcome Center…it's a perfect "home base" for all of your activities in Monteverde.

Hotel Banana Azul in Puerto Viejo

Puerto Viejo de Talamanca, Limon, Costa Rica
(506) 2750 – 2035
www.bananaazul.com
$64 - $223/night

Known for its beauty and charm, this hotel boasts a beautiful garden with hammocks and deck chairs. The staff is friendly and accommodating, and the menu has vegan-friendly options. Bribri culture (a local indigenous tribe) melds with Caribbean traditions to create a charming atmosphere. The hotel also offers multiple adventure packages, including whitewater rafting, canopy tours, and hiking. Free wifi is provided, and a restaurant is attached to the hotel.

Adventure Inn in San Jose

1013 Airport Boulevard
Pan American Highway, Cariari, San Jose, Costa Rica
(506) 2239-2633
http://www.adventure-inn.com/
$77-$128/night

This hotel is a great deal. Free airport shuttles and discounts on tours and other services make this hotel a winner for the traveler wishing to save money. The hotel is modern and large, with a pool and work out amenities. Free long-distance, wi-fi, and breakfast are also provided.

Casa Mariposa in Chirripo

San Gerardo de Rivas, Chirripo National Park, Costa Rica
(506) 2742-5037
http://www.hotelcasamariposa.net
6500 colones-26,000 colones/night

Located only about 50 meters from the trailhead, this is the ideal lodging for backpackers and hikers. A hostel with communal kitchens and bathrooms, it's perfect for those needing a place to stay before and after hiking the peak. The owners will even store your other luggage for free while you're climbing!

Places to Eat & Drink

Local fare can be purchased from "sodas," small affordable shops found throughout Costa Rica. But if you're interested in restaurants, there are plenty available. Tourism has brought culinary influences from all over the world, and there's no end to the variety of tastes. Here are some of the most highly recommended restaurants in various cities throughout Costa Rica.

Jardin del Parque in San Jose

Calle 19, Ave 3era, Casa 172, San Jose 1000, Costa Rica
(506) 2248 – 4979
https://www.facebook.com/JardinDelParque
CAD8 – CAD12

Known for its vegetarian fare, this restaurant will delight people of all tastes. Outdoor seating is available, and they also deliver. The view of the park and the affordable freshness of the food make this spot a regular stop for locals.

Stashus con Fusion in Puerto Viejo

200 meters south of town, next door to soda Elena Brown, Costa Rica
(506) 2750 – 0530
CAD7 – CAD15

This restaurant is a popular spot because if its delicious fusion of Latin, Asian and Caribbean flavors—the perfect representation of the little town of Puerto Viejo itself! The fish tacos are legendary, and the décor consists of local artwork. Visitors love the funky and open atmosphere, and the service is excellent.

Restaurante Tico y Rico Monteverde

Main Street, Santa Elena, Monteverde Cloud Forest Reserve, Costa Rica
(506) 8815 – 0520
Average $20 for two main courses and two drinks.

Excellent food and excellent service make this restaurant a favorite for those staying in Monteverde, and the prices are some of the best in the area. Families with children have found this restaurant especially accommodating, and people of all ages have loved the open atmosphere.

Wild Ginger in Torguguero

150 meters north of the Primary School, Beachfront Path, Tortuguero, Costa Rica
(506) 2709 – 8240
http://wildginger.freevar.com/
CAD4 – CAD16

For those seeking Caribbean and California Fusion, this is a gem off the beaten path. The staff is friendly, the food creative, and best of all, the restaurant is open late and is famous for its mixed drinks. Offering high-end food for reasonable prices, this eatery has something for everyone.

Cascajo's del Arenal

800 meters west of Hotel Tabacon, Arenal Volcano National Park, Costa Rica
(506) 2479 – 9674
$7 - $15

A great place to get a taste of local cuisine, this small restaurant serves big portions for reasonable prices. It may look like an unassuming local "soda," but one bite of the food and you'll know it stands out from the rest. The staff is friendly and you can even enjoy a view of the volcano while you eat! Be sure to try some of the local fresh fish.

Places to Shop

Whether you're staying in bustling San Jose or hopping from small beach town to beach town, there are always great shopping opportunities. Many tourist destinations are filled with small stands offering local goods, and these are some of the best places to pick up souvenirs and gifts. Cash is always recommended, as many local vendors may not accept cards, although travelers are advised to carry cash securely. Haggling and bargaining is expected.

Mercado Central in San Jose

The market was established in 1880, and occupies and entire block on Avenida Central, 250 meters north of

Parque Central. It consists of a series of complex alleys with over 200 shops. This is the place to find everything from inexpensive t-shirts, fresh meats and vegetables, spices, flowers, and souvenirs. Items are reasonably priced, although visitors should feel free to haggle with the local vendors, as always. It can be crowded, though — tens of thousands of people visit the market every day.

Mercado Nacional de Artesanías in San Jose

A great resource to find local arts and crafts, this is the place to go if you are a lover of beauty. Woodwork is popular, and travelers delight in the rosewood boxes set with tiny hand-painted tiles. The best way to get to Mercado Artesania is to grab a taxi and ask for the Plaza del Democracia on 2nd Avenue. While prices may be slightly higher, the goods are of higher quality. This is also a great place to buy some of the best local coffee in the world.

Multiplaza Mall in San Jose

Located next to Hotel Intercontinental, this is a great place to find everything from goods (clothes, jewelry, groceries) to services (beauty parlors, restaurants, movie theaters). Comparable to a United States shopping mall, prices range from low to high. The Multiplaza Mall is a franchise that exists throughout Central America, and the San Jose location is a hotspot for local shoppers and tourists alike.

Roadside Market in Puerto Viejo

Located along the main beach road, this is a perfect place to find jewelry, beads, and other local craftwork. The Bohemian flavor of this town is evident in the wares available for sale, and you may even find some unique, original artwork! Bargaining is expected, and visitors should be sure to walk the streets to find the best prices before buying.

Santa Elena Souvenir Shops in Monteverde

If you're looking for souvenirs or gifts, Monteverde has some of the best prices in the country. If you're traveling through the country, most travelers recommend waiting until Monteverde to buy souvenirs and gifts. The main souvenir shop in Santa Elena is also attached to a supermarket, so feel free to pick up a few pieces of fruit or local bread to enjoy while you shop!

Printed in Great Britain
by Amazon.co.uk, Ltd.,
Marston Gate.